THE
CATALYST
OF
CONFIDENCE

THE
CATALYST
OF
CONFIDENCE

*A Simple and Practical
Guide to Understanding
Human Potential*

KEN PARSELL

THE CATALYST OF CONFIDENCE

PUBLISHED BY
Parsell Enterprise Group

Copyright © 2011 by Ken Parsell

All rights reserved. No part of this publication may be reproduced, distributed, or transmitted in any form or by any means, including photocopying, recording, or other mechanical or electronic methods, without the prior written permission of the author, except in the case of brief quotations embodied in critical reviews and certain other non-commercial uses permitted by copyright law. For permission requests, write to the author at the address below.

Parsell Enterprise Group
P.O. Box 901
Brighton, MI 48116
Fax: (877) 216-5032   Email: info@kenparsell.com

Printed in the United States of America

Cover design and layout by Ken Parsell
Posterior quote by James Allen

ISBN: 978-0615451343
First Edition, March 2011 (Paperback)

Get articles, case studies and ask questions at
www.catalystofconfidence.com

"Thinking is the hardest work there is, which is probably why so few people engage in it."

-Henry Ford

Table of Contents

Preface . . . . *xi*

Introduction . . . . *xv*

I	The Foundation of the World 19
II	The Moratorium of Choice 29
III	The Seeds of Reality 37
IV	Of Mice and Men 45
V	The Motor of the World 55
VI	In Profit of Nothing 63
VII	The Greatest Lie Ever Told 71
VIII	The Imp of Deception 81
IX	Maximum Overdrive 91
X	The Philosophy of Power 99
XI	The Catalyst of Confidence 107
XII	The World's Your Oyster 115

Formulas 123

Laws 127

Lexicon 133

Sources 145

To My Wife

Preface

"On this path, it is only the first step that counts."

-*Jean-Marie Vianney*

Overview and Acknowledgments

Preface

A little over a year ago I found myself sitting in a living room with a very close friend. We were discussing the outline to a manuscript I was about to begin writing. I had slowly been piecing the project together for years from material I was teaching in classes and workshops. It was time to make the leap from mental to physical, from idea to reality. My main goal was keeping the content simple. I believe the genius of an idea is not seen in its complexity, but in its simplicity and applicability. In other words, I wanted the book to be easy to understand and simple to apply. I wanted it to be practical. I believe it is.

You will find the chapters or "lessons" quite short and easily readable. All lessons are composed of facts, contain very little "fluff," and have been specifically designed to provoke thought and analysis. I have included a "selected quotes" section at the end of each lesson to support its general idea. There are also sections dedicated to helping the reader understand his or her tendencies regarding each topic and numerous formulas and laws exist throughout the book (which can also be found in the appendix). A lexicon has also been added to help readers understand the semantics of the book.

I would like to thank my wife, Cindy, for her constant support and unerring faith in me. I would also like to thank my great friend, Michael "Ollie" Wiitala. This book would not have been possible without his tremendous insight and analysis.

Ken Parsell
January 2011

Introduction

*"Knowing is not enough; we must apply.
Willing is not enough; we must do."*

-Goethe

Intellectual and Functional Understanding

Introduction

Confidence stems from our capacity to *acknowledge* and *understand* the reality of human potential. To acknowledge is simply to recognize something. To understand, however, requires a more complete explanation. When we hear the term "understanding" we often interpret it as comprehending something *intellectually,* and for the most part, this is how "understanding" is generally perceived. But for us to truly *understand* human potential we must do more than conceptualize it intellectually.

The Dichotomy of Understanding

A proper perspective on the word "understanding" takes into account a kind of duality of meaning. On one hand we have the intellectual or "theoretical" understanding of a subject. On the other we have the functional or "practical" understanding, i.e., learning by doing. Both components are necessary to fully *understand* a given subject. Stated simply, to truly understand human potential we must understand it on both an intellectual *and* functional basis.

The "Understanding" Formula

Intellectual + Functional = Understanding (Complete)

How To Understand This Book

The information contained in this book provides us with the *intellectual* components needed to understand human potential. The *functional* components, however, may only be attained through the *application* of this information, i.e., your ability to *actively* incorporate each lesson into your daily life. Functional understanding is the fruit of your ability to *apply* what you have intellectually learned.

Understanding The Reality of Human Potential

Incorporating the subsequent lessons into your life can be challenging, but it's well worth it. The benefits of understanding your potential will last a lifetime and should not be easily dismissed or underestimated. Your life is an opportunity held in the palm of your hand, and what you do with it is largely dependent on you. Always remember that it is only through *applying* what you learn that you may truly come to *understand* your potential and thereby unlock *The Catalyst of Confidence*.

The Laws of Intellectual and Functional Understanding

1. Genuine understanding is comprised of both intellectual and functional components.

Understanding Your Tendencies

1. Do you *apply* what you learn or simply try to "remember" it?
    - What can you do to *actively apply* the information you intellectually understand?

The Foundation of the World

"What lies beyond us and what lies before us are tiny matters when compared to what lies within us."

-Ralph Waldo Emerson

Lesson I: Perception and Belief

The Foundation of the World

The history of humanity is the history of human belief. The achievements of our past, present and future have been, are, and will be, built by what we *believe* is possible. From the ancient pyramids, to the great cathedrals, from skyscrapers reaching to the heavens, to the man on the moon, the beliefs of human beings have created the reality of our world. Without belief, nothing is possible. Nothing could change or progress, our lives would stagnate and human beings as we know them would not exist. Everything begins with belief. Beliefs are the foundation of the world.

The Ultimate Premise

The first lesson is, in essence, the premise of each lesson contained in this book. Belief creates meaning. Without belief, truths and principals become null and void. For instance, without the *belief* that you control your own actions, you will not consciously control them. Without the *belief* that failure is a building block of success, you will be terrified to fail. Without the *belief* that you can change your habits, you will be powerless in changing them. Actions *presuppose* belief.

Your Beliefs Determine Your Perception of Reality

Your beliefs determine your perception of reality. When you believe something is true, you act as though it is true, regardless of whether or not it actually is. It is because we act on the basis of our beliefs that we (almost always) produce evidence that support our beliefs. For instance, a child who *believes* she is "stupid" or "learning disabled" will almost always find "proof" on her report card. This "proof" naturally reinforces her belief that she can't learn or isn't competent in school. But is she really incapable of learning or does she simply *believe* she is? Her beliefs have determined her perception of reality and her perception of reality governs her actions.

Your Beliefs Determine Your Potential

Your beliefs not only define your reality, they also determine what you are capable of doing. The athlete who *believes* she has reached her limit—has. The businessman who *believes* he can double his annual growth—can. Belief gives you the power to *do*. When you believe you can do something the *how-to-do-it* develops naturally.* It is rarely a question of how, but more often a question of: *Do I believe I can?* Belief, however, does not guarantee results. Believing you can accomplish something is no guarantee that you *will*, but it does mean you *could*. It is your *belief* which makes something *possible*. What you *believe* you can do will determine what you are capable of doing.

You Create Your Beliefs

Your beliefs have been created by you. Despite the fact as children we do not *consciously* choose what to believe, we still develop beliefs. Again, the child who believes she is "stupid" or "learning disabled" did not consciously choose to believe such things. Such beliefs may have resulted from what she has been told by a teacher, her parents or perhaps what she has communicated to herself upon seeing her report card. As we mature, however, we should develop the awareness that our beliefs are a choice. You can *choose* to develop beliefs that limit you

---
* This concept is discussed in detail in *Lesson III*.

just as easily as you can *choose* to develop beliefs which strengthen your abilities. The opinions of other people do not have to become your reality. No one has the power to force you to believe anything: the choice is your own.

The Creation of Beliefs

A belief is the result of the perception and repetition of information. Specifically, our beliefs are created in three separate steps:
1. Perception
2. Repetition
3. Belief

1. Perception: Information enters our minds through our senses where it is immediately interpreted by how we think. We call this perception because the *substance* of this information is irrelevant: what matters is how we *perceive* it. As an example, let us assume the child who currently believes she is "stupid" or "learning disabled" had previously failed a test. Upon discovering her result, the substance of this information, unbiased, as it first entered her mind, would have been: *I failed the test*. However, if she *currently* believes she is "stupid," her initial perception of her failure was most likely: "I failed the test, *therefore I must be stupid*." She may have failed the test, but her perception of failing was the first step in creating her belief. At this point, her perception does not yet govern her behavior.

2. Repetition: Before perceived information may become a belief, it must be reinforced through repetition. Repetition is the catalyst of belief. The brain simply believes what you repeatedly tell it, regardless of whether or not it happens to be true. Before the child's perception of failure may become a belief, it must be reinforced through repetition, i.e., she must repeat to herself: *"I failed the test; I must be stupid"* over and over again. She may continue to communicate this to herself whenever she makes a mistake or receives a poor grade. These constant "suggestions" reinforce her perception that *she is stupid*. Her reinforced perceptions are beginning to influence her behavior; she is beginning to *expect* poor grades.

3. Belief: After a perception has been reinforced over time, it becomes a belief. At some point, after the child has reinforced her perception often enough, she no longer needs to consciously tell herself *"I am stupid."* Her perception will become subconscious—becoming part of her *self-image*—becoming part of *who she thinks she is*. The child's perception is now a belief: an internal representation that governs her behavior. As a result, she behaves like a student who cannot academically learn—a student *who is learning disabled*. Her *belief* determines the choices she makes, the actions she takes, and the results she creates.

The Belief Formula

Information → Perception → Repetition → Belief

Your Beliefs Are Liquid

Your beliefs are not fixed, they are liquid, they can be changed and reshaped at will. If you don't like your beliefs: change them! This is accomplished using the same three steps which created them in the first place:
1. Change your perception.

2. Reinforce your new perception through repetition.
3. Over time, your new perception will become a belief.

Your Beliefs Determine Your Self-Image

Your self-image is a psychological blueprint of yourself. It has been created by *what-you-believe-about-you*. It is your opinion of your own value. It is a mental representation of all your beliefs combined. Everything you do or feel, your reality, even the things you are capable of doing, are always aligned with your self-image.

The Self-Image Formula

Beliefs → Self-Image → Reality/Potential

Change Your Beliefs—Change Your Self-Image

We often create a self-image which works against or limits us. Your self-image may be limiting you. It may tell you that you cannot change, that you cannot overcome, that you cannot accomplish. These are simply perceptions of your mind and are only true if you *believe* them to be. Your self-image can be changed. It is the mental representation of the sum total of your beliefs—*beliefs you control—beliefs you can change.* If your self-image is not on your side: change it! In order to change your self-image, simply change your beliefs.

Selected Quotes

"Believe you can succeed and you will."
-David J. Schwartz

The Foundation of the World

"The self-image is a "premise," a base, or a foundation upon which your entire personality, your behavior, and even your circumstances are built."
-Maxwell Maltz

"Well-ordered self-love is right and natural."
-Thomas Aquinas

"It is our belief that determines how much of our potential we'll be able to tap."
-Anthony Robbins

"To have faith is to be sure of the things we hope for, to be certain of the things we cannot see."
-Hebrews 11:1

The Laws of Perception and Belief

1. Actions presuppose belief.
2. Beliefs are created, strengthened and nurtured by oneself.
3. Beliefs govern action.
4. Beliefs determine one's perception of reality.
5. Beliefs determine one's potential.
6. Beliefs may be changed.
7. Beliefs are developed and changed through the perception and repetition of information.

Understanding Your Tendencies

1. Do you believe every problem has a solution?
2. What do you believe about yourself?
3. Do your beliefs build you up or tear you down?
4. How often do you say you can't do something?

The Foundation of the World

5. If you succeed do you call it luck?
6. How do you perceive what happens to you?
7. Do you believe in yourself?
8. Have you allowed other people to determine what you believe about yourself?
9. What have you done to change limiting beliefs?
10. Why do you believe what you believe?

The Moratorium of Choice

"Unlike the cruel Leonidas who demanded that you stand: I require only—that you kneel."

-Xerxes, from the motion picture "300"

Lesson II: Choice and Initiative

The Moratorium of Choice

Numerous speculations have been made which conclude that human choice is an illusion. What is referred to as "free will" is actually a conditioned physical response to external stimuli. In other words, your behavior is determined by your environment, there is no free will and you are no better than an animal. You do not control your actions, your environment does. Your failures are not your fault and anything you accomplish is the result of chance. This is the moratorium of choice—it is a lie.

Everything You Do Is A Choice

Whether you believe it or not, you possess the ability to control your own actions. You control you. Your actions are the result of your choices. You are where you are today because of the choices you made yesterday. Where you are tomorrow will be determined by the choices you make today. Your life is the composite result of your own choices. While certain behaviorist may hail the death of "free will" on the premise that a given stimulus will produce a given response, they fail to note that between that stimulus and response, we have the freedom to choose. Everything you *do* is a choice.

The Volition Formula

$$\text{Stimulus} \rightarrow (\text{Choice}) \rightarrow \text{Response}$$

You Determine Your Success or Failure

It is because your choices and actions produce *results* that it can be said that you are the defining factor of your successes and failures. You possess the initiative and the responsibility to solve problems and take action. No other person will work as hard as you to solve your problems. No other person will work as hard as you to reach your goals and dreams. If you fail, you determine how you respond: *do you give up or press on?* Sooner or later you must recognize, "if *it's* to be—it's up to *me*." Personal initiative—your ability to consciously *choose* to take action—can literally change the course of your life. If you wish to be better—*be better*. If you wish to do better—*do better*. If there is a problem in your life—*fix it*. It really is that simple. It is only after you admit that *you* determine your success or failure that you can honestly decide to succeed.

You Cannot Control The World: Only Yourself

You cannot control external circumstances. You can, however, control how you respond to them. We cannot always control what happens to us, but we can control how we respond, and how we respond makes all the difference. Between stimulus and response stands *choice*. Unfortunately, most people are *reactive:* they allow external circumstances to control their behavior. They react to what happens to them instantly, without conscious thought. As a result, their behavior is, for the most part, determined by their physical environment. Reactive people often build their lives and emotions around the conduct of others, allowing other people to control them.

You Are Either Reactive or Active

Ultimately how you respond to external circumstances (what happens to you) is your choice. There are only two options when responding to external circumstances, or as behaviorists call it, stimuli:

1. Reactive
2. Active

1. Reactive: The majority of people are reactive, they allow external circumstances to control their feelings and actions. A reactive response is characterized by a lack of personal accountability. These responses tend to manifest themselves through making excuses, blaming others and fault finding. A reactive response often results in a plethora of harmful emotions, such as a bad attitude, anger or a victim mentality. Reactive responders generally say things such as:
- "It's *not* my fault!"
- "*God* hates me!"
- "*Why* does this always happen to me?!"
- "*Who* did this?!"
- "It's *your* fault I'm acting this way!"

If you look closely, each of these statements emphasizes the transfer of responsibility from oneself to *some other party*. In short, a reactive response does not seek to solve anything, but rather, seeks to justify its position and unknowingly prolong its frustration.

2. Active: Few people respond to external circumstances actively. An active response is characterized by a strong sense of personal accountability while examining what can be done to *improve* the *situation* we are responding to and/or *ourselves*. People who actively respond to life do not blame others or make excuses. They maintain a level attitude and are not angered easily. They can remain calm, cool and collected, despite what is going on around them. Their behavior is the result of their own conscious choice.

This response often results in individuals gaining a greater level of awareness and control over themselves. In pursuit of improving the situation, themselves, or both, active responders often ask themselves questions or make statements such as:
- "It's *my* fault and *I'm* going to fix it."
- "*What* can *I* do to help this situation?"
- "Is this response *really* helping me?"
- "*What* can *I learn* from this situation?"
- "*I'm sorry*, it's *my fault*, what can *I do* to fix it?"
- "*How* can *I change* for the better?"

Notice the difference when compared to the previous "reactive" responses. Active responses do not include excuses, finger pointing or negative statements, but rather, hold the spotlight firmly on the individual (personal accountability) and focus on solving the problem and/or improving oneself.

The Response Formula

      External Circumstances → Reactive or Active

Selected Quotes

    "I am master of my fate I am captain of my soul."
                                        -Henley

          "Don't find fault, find a remedy."
                      -Henry Ford

"It's not what happens to you, it's how you handle it."
                                      -Anonymous

The Moratorium of Choice

"Circumstance does not make us;
it reveals us to ourselves."
-James Allen

"If freedom is to be had by men, it is to come
at the price of responsibility."
-Anonymous

"A man sooner or later discovers that he is the master-
gardener of his soul, the director of his life."
-James Allen

"Don't look to the stars for the cause of your misfortunes,
look to yourself to get better results."
-Napoleon Hill

"Everyone thinks of changing the world, but
no one thinks of changing himself."
-Leo Tolstoy

"A man has free choice to the extent that he is rational."
-Thomas Aquinas

"Men are anxious to improve their circumstances,
but are unwilling to improve themselves;
they therefore remain bound."
-James Allen

"He who controls others may be powerful, but
he who controls himself is mightier still."
-Lao Tsu

The Moratorium of Choice

> *"The very fact that you are a complainer, shows that you deserve your lot."*
> -James Allen

The Laws of Choice and Initiative

1. Individuals possess the ability to take action: to solve problems and direct their life.
2. Everything one does is a choice.
3. Through choice and action individuals determine their success and failure.
4. Between stimulus and response is choice.
5. Choice determines one's response to external circumstances.

Understanding Your Tendencies

1. Do you rely on other people to solve your problems for you?
2. Have you allowed other people to determine your behavior or mental attitude?
3. Are you inclined to make excuses or blame other people?
4. How do you respond when things don't go your way?
5. What have you learned from solving your own problems?
6. Is your happiness dependent on someone or something else?
7. Are you working toward a goal or dream?
8. Do you ever complain?
9. When you make mistakes are you likely to admit it?
10. Do you *believe* you can control your actions?

The Seeds of Reality

*"I know of no more encouraging fact than the
unquestionable ability of man to elevate
his life by a conscious endeavor."*

-Henry David Thoreau

Lesson III: Goals and Dreams

All human advancements, inventions, innovations, successful marriages or social progresses of any kind, have a starting point. It is our ability to *conceive,* beyond our immediate reality, that defines the starting point of our achievements. Dreams are the seeds of realities. Nurtured and fed, they produce, cut off and starved, they die. The sole focus of this lesson is dedicated to providing a simple, step-by-step process, that gives you the necessary understanding to bring your ideas and dreams into reality.

Thoughts Are The Seeds of Reality

All significant achievements have been created twice. First in the mental (thought) world, and second in the physical (material) world. This first cause or "mental creation" is the starting point of all achievement; it is the process of defining what it is you want, and seeing it (visualizing) as if it were actually happening.

The Necessity of Desire

All accomplishments presuppose a *desire* to accomplish. Without a *burning desire* to reach an objective, we will—more often than not—fail. It is our *desire* which provides us with the ability to *persist* through the steps needed to accomplish our goals.

From Dreams to Reality

Thoughts, ideas and dreams become reality through the consistent application of five steps:
   1. Define
   2. Focus
   3. Believe

4. Plan
5. Act

1. Define Your Objective: If you want to accomplish something, the first thing you must do is define it. Write out a statement containing exactly what you wish to accomplish and describe it in specific detail. At this time, it is not important that you know *how* to accomplish the object of your desire.

2. Focus On Your Objective: After you have defined (in writing) what it is you want and described it in specific detail, you must begin concentrating on the very thing you have defined. Just as a garden must be cared for, weeded and watered by its owner, so does the object of your desire require your *consistent* attention and *concentration* if it is to *become reality*. To adequately concentrate on your objective read *aloud* your written statement a minimum of twice daily. While reading your statement *aloud*, see (visualize) and feel (emotionalize) yourself actually accomplishing the object of your desire.

3. Give Your Mind Time To Believe: Just as the mind comes to *believe* our perceptions which are reinforced *over time* so to does the mind respond to your spoken statements and emotionalized visualizations. Eventually your mind will have no choice but to *believe* you can accomplish your objective and will immediately begin searching for ways to bring the object of your concentration into reality. You will begin thinking in terms of *how* you can accomplish your goal. Your mind will become magnetized toward the object of your desire and will literally begin "working out" ways to help you achieve it.

4. Define Your Plan: Continue reading your statement *aloud* while *seeing* and *feeling* yourself accomplishing the object of your desire. Over time you will begin to notice ideas in your mind, appearing "out of nowhere." Many of these ideas will involve a method of *how* to accomplish your objective. Begin writing down these ideas as they appear in your mind, and over time, workout a plan, in writing, which details exactly how you will accomplish your goal, and includes the length of time expected for its attainment.

5. Act On Your Plan: Act *immediately* on the plan you have developed in writing! Often times our plans may prove to be faulty and not work as we had expected. It is of no importance if the initial plan you develop does not work. You may always change and improve your plans! If you continue to concentrate upon the object of your desire new ideas for its attainment will continue to appear in your mind. Always be open to new ideas as they develop!

The Dream Formula

Define → Focus → Believe → Plan → Act
(Mental Creation → Material Creation)

The Joy of Endeavor

The hope of future achievement in pursuit of a definite objective is among the greatest of life's pleasures. The most notable benefit of pursuing a purpose is the fact that those who *actively* pursue their dreams are not influenced by the trifles of everyday life; they literally do not notice problems, they are consumed by the desire to create beyond their immediate reality. Only those who have no purpose in life easily become the victim of petty worries, fears, troubles, gossips, and self-pity.

The Voice of Critics

When you undertake to accomplish anything beyond mediocrity, you will be criticized, often by those closest to you. You will be told "you can't do it," or "it isn't going to work," or "why can't you just be like everyone else?" or "what makes you think you can do something like that?" Some people will honestly be concerned about you while others may feel threatened by you and will do anything in their power to convince you to give up. Perhaps a response cannot be better exemplified than by U.S. President Theodore Roosevelt:

> *It is not the critic who counts: not the man who points out how the strong man stumbles or where the doer of deeds could have done better. The credit belongs to the man who is actually in the arena, whose face is marred by dust and sweat and blood, who strives valiantly, who errs and comes up short again and again, because there is no effort without error or shortcoming, but who knows the great enthusiasms, the great devotions, who spends himself for a worthy cause; who, at the best, knows, in the end, the triumph of high achievement, and who, at the worst, if he fails, at least he fails while daring greatly, so that his place shall never be with those cold and timid souls who knew neither victory nor defeat.*

Selected Quotes

"If one advances confidently in the direction of his dreams...he will meet with a success unexpected in common hours."
-Henry David Thoreau

"Life is a daring bold adventure, or nothing."
-Helen Keller

"Deprived of meaningful work, man and women lose their reason for existence, they go stark, raving mad."
-Fyodor Dostoevsky

"Most men are dead at age 20 and wait until age 70 to be buried."
-Benjamin Franklin

"I saw the angel in the marble and I chiseled until I set it free."
-Michelangelo

"The mass of men lead lives of quiet desperation."
-Henry David Thoreau

"He who has a why to live can bear almost any how."
-Friedrich Nietzsche

"First they ignore you, then they laugh at you, then they fight you, then you win."
-Mahatma Ghandi

> *"Doing what you love is the cornerstone
> of having abundance in your life."*
> *-Wayne Dyer*

> *"The greater danger for most of us is not that our
> aim is too high and we miss it, but that
> it is too low and we reach it."*
> *-Michelangelo*

The Laws of Goals and Dreams

1. All things begin as thoughts.
2. All accomplishment presupposes desire.
3. The starting point of all achievement is defining what one wants.
4. All objectives are realized through the conscious or unconscious application of a five-step process.

Understanding Your Tendencies

1. Do you have goals and dreams?
2. What are you *currently* working to accomplish?
3. Have you defined your goals and dreams in writing?
4. Do you consistently focus on your defined goals?
5. Have you given your mind the necessary time to begin working out plans for your goals?
6. After you develop plans, how long do you wait before acting on them?
7. What does your *ideal* life look like?
8. If you could do anything, what would you do?
9. Do you realize the mental process of bringing goals and dreams into reality can be used to solve personal problems?

Of Mice and Men

"Human beings, by changing the inner attitudes of their minds, can change the outer aspects of their lives."

-William James

Lesson IV: Thought and Concentration

The ability to recognize and use the power of our mind and to direct that power toward a specific purpose is perhaps the greatest asset we possess. Our mind is like a garden, which we may cultivate intelligently or allow to run wild. If nothing useful is *planted* within it, nothing useful will *grow* out of it and it will soon be overgrown with weeds. This ability, to recognize and use the power of our mind, is the defining factor of wishes and dreams, of misery and happiness, and of mice and men.

Information: The Language of Your Mind

Your mind operates according to the *information* you associate with and concentrate upon. Information is *any input* which enters the *conscious mind* through the five senses (seeing, hearing, tasting, touching, smelling) or by some other means of communication.

The Substance of Information

Information which enters your mind may be classified as:
1. Positive
2. Negative

1. Positive: Information which improves your life, helps solve problems, or increases your ability to accomplish goals and dreams.

2. Negative: Information which does not improve your life, causes or prolongs problems, or hinders your ability to accomplish goals and dreams.

Information and Environment

The information we associate with is largely derived from our environment, which as adults, we can actively control. Every person we associate with, every TV show we watch, every book we read, every song we listen to, everything we do—is feeding information to our mind. It is often this information which determines our thought process and thereby lays the groundwork of our lives.

Information Is Subordinate To Perception

As previously mentioned in *Lesson I: Perception and Belief*, the substance of information, as it first appears in your mind, is irrelevant: what matters is *how you perceive it*. In other words, the information you associate with—or concentrate upon—may be objectively positive or negative, *but it is still subordinate to your perceptions*. Your perceptions give you the power to change negatives into positives and positives into negatives. It's not about what happens to you, it's about *how you perceive what happens to you*.

Concentration and Dominating Thoughts

The information we concentrate upon determines our dominating thoughts. Dominating thoughts are to be understood as the information we think in terms of and/or make decisions based on. We develop *belief* in whatever we repeat to ourselves, regardless if what we communicate is true or false. If we repeat a lie over and over we will eventually accept the lie and *believe* it to be true. In a similar manner, any thought which is repeatedly concentrated upon, will—over time—attract to it other similar or related thoughts, *be they positive or negative.* These repeated thoughts *or* thoughts which are *emotionalized* create a "magnetic" force which attract similar or related thoughts to our mind. Such magnetized thoughts may be compared to a seed which, when planted, grows and multiplies itself over and over until finally, it represents the dominating thoughts we hold in our mind.

The Information Formula

Information → Thinking*

Dominating Thoughts Determine Action and Behavior

It is because we think in terms of, and make decisions on the basis of, our dominating thoughts, that we are able to understand the origins of our actions and behavior. All action springs from thought and we eventually become synonymous with the information we associate with and concentrate upon. We have literally become who we are because of the *dominating thoughts* we have held in our minds. We find that people who repeatedly associate with —or concentrate upon—negative information, tend to behave in a negative way, which can often be seen in a bad attitude, constant complaining, criticizing, or a victim mentality. In the same manner, individuals who associate with information of a positive nature tend to behave in ways much more conducive to accomplishing their goals and dreams. In short, we "act out" the information we concentrate upon. What we think about we bring about through our actions. This is why having positive role-models or personal heroes can be so powerful, because we

---

* The information you associate with or concentrate upon determines your thinking, i.e., your dominating thoughts.

naturally emulate the qualities we admire and focus our minds upon.

The Thought/Action Formula

$$\text{Information} \rightarrow \text{Thinking} \rightarrow \text{Action}$$

The Brain[*] Cannot Distinguish Between Real and Imagined Experiences

Our physical brain has no way of differentiating between "real" experiences and fantasies. As far as our brain is concerned, all mental activity *is* reality and actually occurred. This is why many athletes are trained to visualize or "see" themselves performing flawlessly as a form of practice. Similarly, if we "see" ourselves as a person who is, say, dishonest, untrustworthy or unattractive, we will literally, over time, become that person. If we see ourselves as an honest, likeable, or capable person, over time, we will develop into a person with those qualities. We should always concentrate on or "see" ourselves as the person we would like to be.

You Are Master of Your Dominating Thoughts

It is within your power to control the information you associate with and concentrate upon. Develop an aware-

---

[*] The term "brain" refers to the physical organ and the unique activity of the nervous system, which should be understood as separate from one's consciousness. When actions are performed the brain comes alive with "electrochemical" activity. When it is said the brain cannot distinguish between what is real and imagined, it is because the same neurological activity occurs within the brain regardless of whether or not an action is physically performed or visualized.

ness of your dominating thoughts and begin to identify them as helpful or harmful to your best interest. If you determine your dominating thoughts are working against you, change the information you associate with, i.e., change your environment or change the information you concentrate upon! Seek information that inspires and helps you. By changing the information you associate with and concentrate upon, you change the person you are becoming and if you can change the person you are, you can determine the person you become.

Selected Quotes

"The invisible part of your life will always impact the visible."
-Lt. Gen. Hal Moore

"Our life is what our thoughts make it. A man will find that as he alters his thoughts toward things and other people, things and other people will alter towards him."
-James Allen

"If man makes himself a worm he must not complain when he is trodden upon."
-Immanuel Kant

"You will become as small as your controlling desire; as great as your dominant aspiration."
-James Allen

"A man is what he thinks about all day long."
-Ralph Waldo Emerson

"Fill your minds with those things that are good and that deserve praise: things that are true, noble, right, pure, lovely, and honorable."
-Philippians 4:8

The Laws of Thought and Concentration

1. The mind is one's greatest asset.
2. The mind operates according to the information it concentrates upon.
3. Individuals are continuously influenced by their environment.
4. The substance of information is positive or negative.
5. Information is subordinate to perception.
6. Dominating thoughts result from the information an individual concentrates upon.
7. Action and behavior is the result of one's dominating thoughts.
8. Individuals emulate the qualities they admire and concentrate upon.
9. Individuals possess the ability to control the information they associate with.

Understanding Your Tendencies

1. Who are you today compared to the person you would like to be tomorrow?
2. What do you concentrate on?
3. What are you thankful for?
4. Who do you see yourself as?
5. Do the people you associate with help you become a better person?
6. Do the people you associate with help you

accomplish your dreams?
7. What type of music do you listen to?
8. What type of TV shows do you watch?
9. What type of books do you read?
    - Do these associations help you improve or accomplish your dreams?
10. What do you think when someone insults you?

The Motor of the World

"We are what we repeatedly do. Excellence, then, is not an act, but a habit."

-Aristotle

Lesson V: Action and Habit

How do you ride a bike? Ask someone *how* they ride a bike and listen to their reply. It will most likely fall somewhere along "I just get on it and ride." We can all ride a bike, and yet it seems few of us can actually explain *how* we do it—we just do it. When we tie our shoes, we don't think about it—we just do it. When someone is cut off driving and is thrown into a fit of road rage—they didn't stop and say to themselves "I think I'm going to start honking the horn, screaming at the top of my lungs, spitting on the windshield, communicating in sign language and risk my life speeding miles out of my way to chase down a complete stranger just to let them know how mad I am!" Again—*they just do it.* People are ruled by habit and rightly so. Habits, are the motor of the world.

Habits Defined

Almost everything we do can be classified as a habit. We often don't recognize this because habits are subconscious actions we perform without consciously realizing it. A habit is any action performed without conscious thought. The point which an action is performed subconsciously is the point which it may properly be defined as a habit.

The Subconscious Mind

Habits are created by the subconscious section of the mind which classifies, stores and implements all information held by the conscious mind. Like a computer, the subconscious mind does precisely what it is programmed to do. The programmer of the subconscious is the conscious mind. Together they form a kind of "psychographical" relationship. Stated simply, the conscious mind "writes" code or "thoughts" onto the subconscious, which carries them out, exactly as "written" or "programmed." As an example, think back to how beliefs are created. First, a perception is "held" in the *conscious* mind. It is then repeated and reinforced over time—*consciously.* Finally, the perception has been held and reinforced often enough, it has become automatic, is now a belief, and is now *subconscious*. A belief is nothing but a thought habit.

The Creation of Habits

To create a habit, perform an action over and over again, until it becomes second nature—that's it! Habits describe any action performed without conscious thought. Habits result from the repetition of *any action,* mental or physical. Actions must be executed *consciously* until the subconscious mind "learns" or is "programmed" and may then perform automatically (subconsciously) without need to inform the conscious section of the mind.

The Amoral Mind

The subconscious mind is amoral: it is not guided by a morality of any nature. The subconscious mind functions based on the information provided by the conscious. It creates patterns of thought and physical habits without any regard to a moral compass. It has no sense of right or wrong, good or bad. It simply does what it is told to do.

The Dichotomy of Habit

Habits may be mental or physical. Thought patterns, ways of thinking or emotional responses are, in essence, mental habits. Physical habits would include riding a bike, tying your shoes, shifting a manual transmission or brushing your teeth. It is also possible for a habit to be both mental and physical. Let us say when someone insults you—you habitually get angry—and when angry, you often exhibit the tendency to pick up and throw the nearest object. The anger, is a mental habit or habitual response to being insulted. The throwing of an object, is a habitual physical response to the mental state of being angry. Both are habits, in this case, performed simultaneously.

The Motor of Your World

Though habits are subconscious actions, they are still actions, and as such they produce *results*. It is because of this that we can say that everyone is a product of their habits. Ultimately, it is your habits that will make or break you. The best of the best in anything, are what they are and where they are, because they have developed habits conducive to being the best. Control and master your habits and they will place the world at your feet. Allow them to run wild and undisciplined and they will destroy you. The most miserable people alive, are who they are, because they have failed to utilize the great power of their habits. A good life is the result of consciously developed habits. Develop useful habits and eliminate and replace all others.

The Habit Formula

Action (Mental/Physical) → Habit → Result (You/Life)

The Complete Formula

Information → Thinking → Actions → Habits → Results

Change Your Actions—Change Your Habits

Habits can be changed. To change your habits, change your actions. A destructive habit cannot simply be willed away, it must be replaced. In other words, a new action must take the place of the old one. To accomplish this, determine the destructive action, which is the habit you would like to remove. When you are about to perform this action, rather than performing it again, perform the action you wish to develop in its place. Continue to perform the desired action at the appropriate time, until it finally, through repetition, becomes a habit.

Develop an Awareness of Your Habits

It can be very challenging to identify our habits. Primarily because they are always performed subconsciously. To develop an awareness of our habits we need to cultivate a sense of our actions, i.e., a sense of what we are doing at any given time. This sense is necessary to: 1) develop an awareness of our habits, and 2) to determine if our habits are destructive or benign. We may need the help of others (outside observers) to identify our habits, particularly those of a destructive nature. When adverse habits are identified, begin working immediately to replace them.

Selected Quotes

"Good habits formed at youth make all the difference."
-Aristotle

"Excellence is an art won by training and habituation. We do not act rightly because we have virtue or excellence, but we rather have those because we have acted rightly."
-Aristotle

"It seems, in fact, as though the second half of a man's life is made up of nothing, but the habits he has accumulated during the first half."
-Fyodor Dostoevsky

"A long habit of not thinking a thing wrong gives it a superficial appearance of being right."
-Thomas Paine

"The beginning of a habit is like an invisible thread, but every time we repeat the act we strengthen the strand, add to it another filament, until it becomes a great cable and binds us irrevocably in thought and act."
-Orison Swett Marden

"A nail is driven out by another nail. Habit is overcome by habit."
-Desiderius Erasmus

The Laws of Action and Habit

1. A habit is an action performed subconsciously.
2. Nearly all actions stem from habit.
3. One's habits result from the repetition of actions.
4. Habits are created and controlled by the subconscious section of the mind.
5. The subconscious mind is not guided by morality.

6. Individuals are the product of their habits.
7. Individuals have the power to change their habits.

Understanding Your Tendencies

1. Have you ever found it hard to change?
2. Have you ever tried to stop doing something, but can't seem to stop?
3. Do you ever say you are going to do something, but don't seem to do it?
4. Are there things other people do that really "tick you off"?
5. Do things which once seemed hard now seem easy?

In Profit of Nothing

"Our doubts are traitors, and make us lose the good we oft might win, by fearing to attempt."

-William Shakespeare

Lesson VI: Fear and Action

It is to dreams what the grim reaper is to mankind. A creeping emotion capable of faltering the greatest of plans. The Achilles heal of life. The harbinger of indecision and procrastination. It is present in nearly every human being at one point or another and in one form or another. It is the most plentiful commodity on earth and it stands to profit you nothing. Its name—Fear.

The Result of Fear

Fear is an emotional state of mind which prevents action. Fear often reveals itself as *indecision, doubt* and *procrastination*, ultimately resulting in *inaction*. Without action, the most vital element of success, nothing can be accomplished and the wheels of human ingenuity stop turning.

Your Habits Create Your Comfort Zone

Every living person has a comfort zone which has been built up from habit. As your beliefs regarding yourself have created your self-image, so have your habits created your "habit-image" or comfort zone. Your comfort zone describes an area of personality which is characterized by *a lack* of anxiety, tension, or fears.

Fear Exists Beyond Your Comfort Zone

By definition, when you move beyond the extent of your comfort zone, you experience an emotion of fear. As an example, when most students begin a new semester, whether in high school or college, they carry a certain amount of anxiety with them to new classes. They are in a new environment with new people. The teacher may require students to perform verbal introductions, etc. For many students, this is a step beyond the limits of their comfort zone. Other students, who may be at ease in such situations, have more developed comfort zones.

The Natural Response to Fear: Avoid It

It is said an ostrich, upon sight of an approaching lion, will respond by burying its head in the sand. The ostrich's motivation, naturally is to avoid the fear of being eaten. If the lion cannot be seen, it must not exist. This is, of course, a myth—yet it describes exactly how most people respond to fear: avoid it. Such actions result in a substantive increase of the fear itself. Avoid a fear and watch as it increases in power over you. Run from a fear and give it the keys to your future. Deny a fear—bury your head in sand—and wait for it to devour you.

Action Conquers Fear

Fear is overcome through action: action conquers fear. Do the thing you fear and the fear disappears. Fail to act or hesitate and the fear increases. Procrastination is the fertile soil in which fear grows. Prompt decision, backed by action (the antithesis of fear), results in the breakdown of the psychological effects of the emotion of fear.

The Fear Formula

$$\text{Action} > \text{Fear}$$

Advice In Conquering Fear

Most of us understand the concept "action conquers fear"

intellectually. It's simple, easy to understand, but in the face of genuine fear, it's easier said than done. We often paralyze ourselves through fear, becoming unable to act in any way whatsoever, thereby vitalizing the fear and giving it greater influence over us. This need not be the case. When confronted by fear of any kind, ask yourself these questions:
1. What am I focused on?
2. What do I believe?
3. What do I see?

1. What Am I Focused On?: When confronted by fear most people focus their attention completely upon the fear itself until it "freaks them out." If you "hold" thoughts of fear in your conscious mind, they will naturally begin producing more thoughts of the same nature. Shift your concentration from fear to *action:* focus on what you can *do*. Instead of concentrating on "I'm *scared* to do this presentation" concentrate on the steps needed to *do* the presentation.

2. What Do I Believe?: Generally if you focus on the actions necessary to do the "presentation," your initial response (in the face of fear) will be: "I can't do it." A mental or verbal "I can't do it" is really a *belief*—and how are beliefs created? Through the perception and repetition of information. The information: doing the presentation, despite fear. The perception: "I can't do it." The most common perception of action (in the face of fear) is "I can't do it!" Change the perception to "I can do it!" and reinforce it.

3. What Do I See?: If you're experiencing fear and anxiety about "doing the presentation," ask, what do you see in your mind? You probably see yourself screwing up, doing a horrible job, people not accepting you, laughing at you, embarrassment, etc. Your *focus* is on your *fear* and you probably *believe* "you can't do it." Shift your concentration from fear to action and begin reinforcing the perception "I can do it." *Then* see (visualize) yourself doing it flawlessly. Visualize yourself going through the motions of completing your presentation with confidence and grace. See yourself succeeding over and over again. Reinforce the perception that *you can do it*, focus your attention on successful actions, and see yourself completing them.

Will utilizing these steps remove your fear? No. The only thing that will remove your fear of "doing the presentation" is *doing the presentation*. These steps are designed to help spur you to action. Act—despite fear—and the fear will disappear.

An Expanded Comfort Zone

The reward of consistent action, despite a fear, is the death of the fear itself. The fear no longer exists in you—your comfort zone has expanded. Every time you take action, despite fears, it expands your comfort zone. Pushing the limits of your comfort zone is how you grow, develop and improve. It provides you with greater ability and talent. Above all, the fruits of an expanded comfort zone can be seen in a more developed self-image and a greater sense of self-reliance.

The Ramifications of Habit

Whether you act despite fear or avoid fears altogether,

your subconscious mind is silently observing behind the scenes. Act consistently over time—despite your fears—and you *will* develop the *habit* of facing your fears (taking action) immediately when you identify them. Avoid your fears and you *will* develop the *habits* of indecision, doubt and procrastination.

Selected Quotes

"Courage is resistance to fear, mastery of fear, not absence of fear."
-Mark Twain

"Unfed worries die of starvation."
-Anonymous

"Action cures fear. Indecision, postponement, on the other hand, fertilize fear."
-David J. Schwartz

"Do the thing you fear and the death of fear is certain."
-Mark Twain

"We gain strength, and courage, and confidence by each experience in which we really stop and look fear in the face...we must do that which we think we cannot."
-Eleanore Roosevelt

"In order to succeed, your desire for success should be greater than your fear of failure."
-Bill Cosby

"Fear doesn't exist anywhere except in the mind."
-Dale Carnegie

The Laws of Fear and Action

1. Fear is an emotional state-of-mind which inhibits one's ability to take action.
2. An individual experiences fear when they move beyond their comfort zone.
3. The more a fear is avoided the more power it has over an individual.
4. Action conquers fear.
5. Overcoming fears expands one's comfort zone.

Understanding Your Tendencies

1. When was the last time you did something that was outside of your comfort zone?
2. Have you ever forced yourself to do something you were afraid to do?
3. Have you ever become mysteriously ill just before you had to do something you were afraid to do?
4. When was the last time you allowed a fear to stop you from doing something?
5. Have you ever experienced "analysis paralysis" as a result of fear?

The Greatest Lie Ever Told

"There is the greatest practical benefit in making a few failures early in life."

-Thomas Henry Huxley

Lesson VII: Failure and Adversity

The Greatest Lie Ever Told

You have learned this from nearly every person you've been in contact with since you were born. You have seen it on television and heard it on the radio; you have read it in newspapers and on the internet; you have observed it in movies and in your personal life. It is not always spoken, but is easily seen in the behavior and attitudes of other people. You have learned to avoid failure—perhaps at all costs. The greatest lie ever told can be summed up in a series of statements we learn from society: *don't fail; don't make mistakes; failure is bad; people who fail are dumb; only stupid people make mistakes; etc.*

Popular Perceptions of Failure

A failure, as popularly defined, refers to an unsuccessful action or failed attempt. People who are consistently unsuccessful are naturally deemed "failures." Both society at large and our education system (including higher education) have shaped our understanding of failure. Chances are you began learning (consciously or not) to avoid failure at a young age. We have been inadvertently taught that good grades reveal the "smarts and successfuls" while poor grades indicate the "stupids and failures." As a result of society's conditioning, the majority of people have adopted similar views about failure:
1. We fear failure.
2. We misunderstand failure.
3. We respond to failure adversely.

1. We Fear Failure: Throughout our lives we have learned to associate failure with being "bad," "stupid," or "inadequate." Who wants to be labeled as "bad" or "stupid?" Our natural response to such associations is the fear of being identified with them.

2. We Misunderstand Failure: As explained above, many of us have learned to associate failure with being "bad," "stupid," or "inadequate." As a result, when we do fail, we often interpret our failure as "proof" that we cannot do something. More often than not, this interpretation provides us with the justification to quit.

3. We Respond To Failure Adversely: No one likes to fail. We all want to be good at whatever it is we choose to do. When we fall short of our expectations we often react negatively with an emotionally charged "sky is falling" mentality.

The Four Stages of Learning

Everything you do has been done as the result of a learning process. This learning process can be summarized in what has been called The Four Stages of Learning:
1. Unconscious Incompetence
2. Conscious Incompetence
3. Conscious Competence
4. Unconscious Competence

1. Unconscious Incompetence: "You don't know how bad you are." You are not yet aware of your incompetence involving a specific activity.

2. Conscious Incompetence: "You know you're bad." You are aware of your incompetence: you have attempted something and failed. This is the point where most people give up or run away.

3. Conscious Competence: "You know you're good." You are aware of your competence, which is the result of persistent action *despite* past failures.

4. Unconscious Competence: "You're so good you can perform without thinking." Your competence has reached a level which allows you to perform a specific action without thinking about it. This final stage is the direct result of the law of habit: You have performed an action successfully, often enough, over time, that you may now perform it without conscious thought (subconsciously).

Process and Product

We are conditioned to see results. We see the expert guitarist. We see the entrepreneur with the "Midas Touch." We see the happily married couple. We see the Olympic Gold Medalist. We see the author or artists' multimillion dollar signing bonus. We see the adroit professor. We see the best of the best in anything. We see the product while failing to see the process they took to become what they are. We fail to see the years of effort and persistence and failure. We do not recognize the discipline, the practice or the time required. Put another way, we observe the best of the best in stage four and fail to realize they began in *stage one*. We glorify the product and disregard the process; yet without the process, the product *cannot exist*.

Persistence Despite Failure Invariably Results In Success

It is through the process of failure that we learn how to succeed. If you desire to be good at anything, you must tolerate being bad when you start *and until you become good*. There isn't a person on earth who didn't fall down when they learned to walk. How did you learn to ride a bike? Did you just get on it and ride or did you fall off over and over until you *learned* to ride?

Visualize Your Success

In *Lesson IV: Thought and Concentration* we learned that our brain* cannot distinguish between real and "imagined" experiences. Visualizing your success provides your brain with a blueprint with which to operate correctly. By "seeing" yourself succeeding you can greatly increase your ability to succeed.

Discourage Failure—Discourage Success

The world glorifies success and achievement while mocking and snickering at those who fail. The ramifications are simple: Discourage failure and you discourage success. If failure is the primary process which results in success why reject it? Failure is the quintessential means of learning. Failure is education. Yet our society punishes it. Why not educate people to better understand it? Is it truly a surprise that so many people are content with doing absolutely nothing with their lives? The person who doesn't fail is the same person who *does nothing*.

Problems Are Opportunities

It has been said that every adversity carries with it the seed of an equal or greater benefit. Every problem you encounter in life carries with it the seed of an opportunity,

---

* As explained in *Lesson IV: Thought and Concentration*, the brain cannot distinguish between what is real and imagined on a neurological level.

The Greatest Lie Ever Told

if you look for it. You can learn something from every unpleasant experience you face. It is often the most trying times in our lives which provide us with the greatest educational experiences.

You Are Not Your Failures

Failure is an event, it is not a person. When you fail, recognize it for what it is, a result, a form of feedback. Understand your failures are not a reflection of your self-worth. This may sound radical, but you can't fail, you can only quit. By disassociating yourself from your failures you change your perspective. Failure, as the world understands it, does not exist. Failure is a perception of the mind. *Failure only exists if it is perceived and accepted as failure.* The perceptual difference between "I failed" and "I am a failure" is disparate. Your choices, actions and habits produce *results*. If the results you have created are not the results you desire, you have two options:
1. Persist (continue toward the results you desire)
2. Quit (accept failure as reality)

Responding to the Popular Perceptions of Failure

As mentioned at the start of this lesson, the majority of people have adopted similar views about failure. In light of the information provided in this lesson, we are better able to address such perceptions:

1. We Fear Failure: Most people develop a fear of being identified with failure because they associate it with being "bad," "stupid," or "inadequate." When we take into account a proper understanding of failure we begin to perceive it for what it is: part of a natural learning process. It is only after we understand the true nature of failure that we can honestly alleviate our fears of being associated with it.

2. We Misunderstand Failure: People generally perceive mistakes or temporary defeats as definitive proof of their inadequacies, resolve they have failed, and quit. Again, in light of the true nature of failure (as a natural learning process) we see that this understanding is fallacious.

3. We Respond To Failure Adversely: In light of The Four Stages of Learning we see that new endeavors nearly always begin with failure. After understanding this truth, early defeats need not be a surprise, but may be accounted for—again—as a natural learning process.

Selected Quotes

"Many of life's failures are men who did not realize how close they were to success when they gave up."
-Thomas Edison

"Every adversity, every failure and every heartache carries with it the Seed of an equivalent or greater Benefit."
-Napoleon Hill

"If the highest aim of a captain were to preserve his ship, he would keep it in port forever."
-Thomas Aquinas

"One of the most common causes of failure is the habit of quitting when one is overtaken by temporary defeat."
-Napoleon Hill

The Greatest Lie Ever Told

"Victory belongs to the most persevering."
-Napoleon Bonaparte

"Failure is not fatal, but failure to change might be."
-John Wooden

"My great concern is not whether you have failed, but whether you are content with your failure."
-Abraham Lincoln

The Laws of Failure and Adversity

1. Failure is the worlds greatest educational process.
2. Persistence despite failure results in success.
3. Visualizing one's success helps one succeed.
4. Problems are opportunities.
5. An individual is not their failures.
6. There is no failure, there are only results.

Understanding Your Tendencies

1. Are you afraid to fail?
2. Have you ever believed that some people were always good at what they do?
3. How do you respond when you fail?
4. Do you let other people's opinions determine what you attempt to do?
5. Can you think of something good that came about as a result of something you initially thought was bad?
6. Do you associate your self-worth with your failures or mistakes?

The Imp of Deception

"The life which is unexamined is not worth living."

-Socrates

Lesson VIII: Self-Deception and Learning

The Imp of Deception 83

Since the dawn of time men and women have competed amongst themselves to establish the best and most skilled. Very little has changed in contemporary culture, indeed competition plays an enormous role in many of our lives. Those of us who have experienced the thrill of competition know first hand the presuppositions we often harbor about our opponents as well as ourselves. We may taunt and berate our adversaries, mistakenly believing our own abilities to be far superior. Such "estimations" generally result in a quick and conclusive defeat and often leave us frustrated and confused. It is upon the reflection of these estimations—specifically those concerning our adversaries and ourselves—where we often find preconceived notions that have been tainted by the imp of deception.

Self-Deception

Self-deception is not solely confined to the world of competition but exists within the context of everyday life. It is perhaps the most sinister form of human ignorance and is commonly defined as "the act of misleading oneself." Essentially, self-deception refers to the betrayal of one's *ultimate* self-interest or *true* potential, in favor of a *perceived* self-interest or potential. Every living person deceives themselves at one time or another and in one way or another. Self-deception poses an eternal question to humankind. It is not a question of whether or not we deceive ourselves, but rather, a question of *what* are we deceived about. We deceive ourselves, and perhaps more often than we are willing to admit. Naturally we may resist such statements, but by definition, we don't always know *when* or *how* we are deceiving ourselves. In fact, a strong case can be made that the person who *believes* they do not suffer from self-deceptions are the most self-deceived of all.

The Face of Self-Deception

Though self-deception is a broad, all-encompassing topic, it generally reveals itself in two distinct areas of our lives:
1. Choices
2. Beliefs

1. Choices: We often deceive ourselves in our decision making, reasoning our choice is for the best, when in reality, it isn't. These so called "deceptions of choice" share a common characteristic: Most involve *choices*, *decisions*, or *actions*, which are based on the fulfillment of an *immediate desire* while simultaneously (consciously or not) ignoring *future consequences*. Some common examples are listed below:
- Procrastination
- Dishonesty
- Denial
- Blind Activity
- Substance Abuse
- Making Excuses
- Promiscuity

An important aspect of "deceptions of choice" which must be considered is the *ramifications of habit*. All choices, decisions, and actions are made under the ever-watchful eye of our subconscious mind, which will (often before we realize it) quickly develop our actions into habits. Suddenly we may find ourselves overwhelmed by a hazardous cycle which can seem near impossible to break.

2. *Beliefs:* Deceptive choices often spring from our *deceptive beliefs*, which are perhaps the more destructive of the two. We often deceive ourselves in our personal beliefs, essentially *believing* something to be true, when in reality it is not. Deceptive beliefs are inherently dangerous because they limit our potential. They create "blind spots" in our thinking and restrict our ability to grow and improve. Some common examples are listed below:
- Arrogance
- Preconceived Notions
- Victim Mentality
- Limiting Beliefs
- Irrational Rigidity

Human nature is a curious thing, particularly when it comes to our own perspectives. We often exhibit an intense bias when it comes to our beliefs and opinions. We are often attached to our opinions, not for any good reason, but simply because they're our own. Nearly all deceptive beliefs are based on the *assumption* that our beliefs and opinions represent the truth or reality of a given circumstance. In other words, deceptive beliefs result from the *unquestioned* premise that our beliefs and opinions are correct.

Identifying Your Deceptions

Known enemies may be fought and defeated, but we cannot solve our problems if we are not aware they exist. The greatest challenge of our deceptions lies in our potential inability to identify them. By definition, our deceptions are *deceptive*, hidden and elusive. They are not always brought into view easily and at times require tremendous effort to identify. In addition, because being self-deceived implies that *we* are the problem, we must be willing to tolerate the short-term emotional discomfort which may come from honestly evaluating ourselves. *We must seek to develop the willingness to change.* As described above, our deceptions reveal themselves in our *choices* and *beliefs*. Some suggestions for identifying our deceptions are described below:

1. Identifying Deceptive Choices: Deceptive choices reveal themselves in the results we create. Actions have consequences. Literally everything you do creates a result, especially over time. It is through the process of reflecting upon *undesirable* results (and specifically the choices and actions which produced them) which enables us to identify our deceptive choices. Deceptive choices are identified through experience. It is commonly said that hindsight is "20/20," and looking back we see the error of our choices very plainly. However, our personal experiences need not be the only mechanism used to identify our deceptive choices. The experience of *others* can also be extremely helpful in avoiding choices and actions which deceive us. We can learn from those who have the *results* we desire and emulate the choices and actions which produced those results.

2. Identifying Deceptive Beliefs: For the most part, deceptive beliefs can also be identified through examining the undesirable results they create. However, the process of identifying deceptive beliefs can be far more subtle and complex than that of identifying deceptive choices. After all, deceptive beliefs are just that: *beliefs*. They are thoughts which have undergone the processes of *Per-*

ception, *Repetition* and *Belief* (as described in *Lesson I: Perception and Belief*), and may have been reinforced for years. They are literally subconscious thought habits—they are part of who we are—they are part of our very being. Needless to say, deceptive beliefs can be incredibly elusive. As previously mentioned, deceptive beliefs result from an *unquestioned assumption* that our beliefs and opinions are correct. With this in mind, not only should we reflect upon our *undesirable* results and experiences, and take into account the experiences of others (as described above), but we must also *question* our beliefs—honestly and vigorously—if we are to identify those which deceive us. We must be brutally honest with ourselves. Most importantly we must seek to identify our own arrogance. We must seek to identify the beliefs and opinions we hold which are not based on facts or rooted in reality. We must ask ourselves: "Why do I believe this?" "What evidence is there that this belief is justified?" "Am I being honest with myself?" Seek to identify the beliefs and opinions which exist simply because you *want* them to. For it is the *baseless* beliefs we defend, which often deceive us the most.

The Reality of Limits

We are limited by what we don't know, acknowledge or realize. In identifying our deceptions we must face the reality that we are not always correct. Knowledge of our faults and shortcomings will often surface and challenge us to grow and improve. It is a stark reminder to us all that *we don't know what we don't know*.

Always Be Open To Learn

The notion that "we don't know what we don't know" provides us with the key to perpetual learning. It reminds us that information does exist, which has not yet been discovered by us. Information which *could* radically alter our perception of reality. We are only limited by our ability to learn, and as such we must maintain the attitude of a *student* in every aspect of our lives. We must approach new information (including the opinions and findings of others) with the attitude of a student. This is not to say you should accept everything you read or hear at face value, but rather, that you should always be open to learn, research and analyze. At best, we may acquire something useful, at worst we may better understand how to approach the often misguided opinions or ideas of other people.

Selected Quotes

"The greatest of faults is to be conscious of none."
-Thomas Carlyle

"He who knows much about others may be learned, but he who understands himself is more intelligent."
-Lao Tsu

"Accept yourself for the person you are and take the actions necessary to become the person you wish to be."
-Anonymous

"Knowing ignorance is strength."
-Lao Tsu

The Imp of Deception

> *"The habitual procrastinator is always an expert creator of alibis."*
> -Napoleon Hill

> *"If we are not true to ourselves we cannot be true to others."*
> -Anonymous

> *"How can you judge others accurately if you have not learned to judge yourself accurately?"*
> -Napoleon Hill

> *"The cleverest of all, in my opinion, is the man who calls himself a fool at least once a month."*
> -Fyodor Dostoevsky

> *"The only true wisdom is knowing you know nothing."*
> -Socrates

The Laws of Self-Deception and Learning

1. Self-deception is the act of misleading oneself.
2. All individuals deceive themselves.
3. Self-deception reveals itself through one's choices and beliefs.
4. Being honest with oneself is critical to identify one's deceptions.
5. Deceptions are identified through reflecting on one's experiences and questioning one's beliefs.
6. There is always more to learn.

Understanding Your Tendencies

1. How often do you reflect on your life (decisions,

thoughts, actions, habits, beliefs, etc.)?
2. Are you ever 100% certain that you are right and someone else is wrong?
3. Do you doubt your own abilities?
4. Are you honest with yourself?
5. Do you ever make excuses to yourself?
6. Do you make decisions based on immediate or long-term desires?
7. Have you ever thought you were better than someone else?
8. Do you ever try to run away from your problems?

Maximum Overdrive

"The world is ruled, and the destiny of civilization is established, by the human emotions."

-Napoleon Hill

Lesson IX: Emotion and Intelligence

Visualize a young man who's heart as been ripped out and walked over by his girlfriend, who has just informed him that their relationship is over and she no longer wants anything to do with him. Observe his drooping posture, his slow and heavy breathing, his head hung low in humiliation. He returns to his home, alone and deeply abased. Before long his sorrow turns to anger and he quickly launches into a tirade of compulsions. The apex of this conniption can be seen when the young man, while lashing out in a fit of rage and frustration, lands a killer blow squarely on the brick wall of his bedroom. The mortar is cracked, the bricks are loose and his hand is broken. He does not yet feel the pain. He does not think clearly. He is running on pure emotion—his mind is operating at maximum overdrive.

The Power of Emotion

Emotions are roughly twenty times more powerful than rational thoughts in influencing our behavior. Imagine a tug-of-war competition where five men hold the rope opposing a hundred. The five represent our logical thought process, the hundred, our emotions. Would you believe the young man from our story came home, sat down on his bed and thought to himself "I think I'll get angry now," "I think I'll start throwing things now," or "I think I'll punch this wall and break my hand"? No—not likely. He did these things because he was overcome with emotion. Emotions are powerful forces in influencing our behavior.

Our Emotional Responses

Emotions are thoughts which are predominantly connected with feelings. Over time we develop a habit of responding to specific emotions in specific ways. As a result, we create neuro-pathways or thought patterns which become automatic. When we feel the emotion of anger, for example, we respond consistently by behaving in a certain way—we may become angry. When we feel the emotion of joy, we again, respond by behaving in a certain way—we may become joyous or good natured. Many people are controlled by their emotions and respond to them impulsively without any conscious thought. Much of our behavior is a habitual response to a given emotion and nearly all of our destructive behavior is an automatic response to a negative emotion.

The Emotion Formula

$$\text{Emotion} \rightarrow \text{Response}$$

Emotional Intelligence Defined

Emotional intelligence can be defined as responding to emotions (especially negative emotions) in ways which benefit us. As children, we had very little control over how we responded to our emotions. We developed the habit of responding to our emotions in childish ways and for the most part these immature responses have been carried by us into our adult lives. As adults, however, we can consciously choose how we respond to our emotions. It is our ability to develop the *habit* of responding to our emotions in ways which benefit us that forms the basis of emotional intelligence.

The Emotional Intelligence Formula

Emotion → (Choice) → Response
(Stimulus → Choice → Response)

Emotional Intelligence Can Be Developed

Emotional intelligence is not something we are born with. It may be true some people naturally possess more emotional intelligence than others, but regardless of our natural endowments, emotional intelligence is a skill that can be developed and cultivated over time. It is based on the law of habit, which is utilized—whether we acknowledge it or not—by every living person.

Developing Emotional Intelligence

Emotional intelligence is the result of the consistent application of two skills:
1. Self-Awareness
2. Self-Management

1. Self-Awareness: Within the context of this lesson, self-awareness is your ability to accurately comprehend your emotions in the moment they occur while understanding your tendency to respond. Self-awareness is developed through consciously making an effort to pay attention to your emotions as they appear and observing your physical and mental reaction to them.

2. Self-Management: Self-management is your ability to respond to your emotions as they occur. It is your ability to consciously respond which gives you the power to develop the habit of responding in beneficial ways.

Developing New Habits

The goal of developing emotional intelligence is developing new habits. Through developing an "awareness" of our emotions as they occur, we are better able to respond to them in ways which benefit us. As described in *Lesson V: Action and Habit*, all actions, over time, produce habits. Emotional intelligence is cultivated by changing the way we *act* in *response* to our *emotions*, in order to develop beneficial habits, and therefore more desirable life circumstances.

Selected Quotes

"I count him braver who overcomes his desires than him who conquers his enemies; for the hardest victory is over self."
-Aristotle

"When dealing with people, remember you are not dealing with creatures of logic, but creatures of emotion."
-Dale Carnegie

"Emotions have taught mankind to reason."
-Luc de Vauvenargues

"Anybody can become angry—that is easy, but to be angry with the right person and to the right degree and at the right time and for the right purpose, and in the right way —that is not within everybody's power and is not easy."
-Aristotle

"The things that we love tell us what we are."
-Thomas Aquinas

The Laws of Emotion and Intelligence

1. Emotions are thoughts linked to feelings.
2. Emotions are powerful forces in influencing one's behavior.
3. Individuals have developed habits in how they respond to their emotions, many of which developed during childhood.
4. Emotional intelligence is the ability to respond to emotions in ways which benefit oneself.
5. Emotional intelligence can be developed.
6. The goal of developing emotional intelligence is to develop new habits.

Understanding Your Tendencies

1. Are you angered easily?
2. Do you throw temper-tantrums, even though you're an adult?
3. Do you hate anyone or does anyone hate you?
4. How do you normally respond when you are overcome with emotions?
5. Have you ever said or done something unintentionally?
   - If you could relive the situation would you respond differently?
6. Do you ever pay attention to your body's physical responses when you are overcome with emotions?
7. Do you have a tendency to overreact when things don't go as planned?

The Philosophy of Power

"The wise man desires to be slow to speak but quick to act."

-~~Confucius~~

Lesson X: Action and Results

We have been told the essence of power is knowledge—that knowledge is power. But is it? We are told to search, learn, explore and discover! We are told to accumulate knowledge. And why not? Knowledge is power! It is upon closer inspection, however, that we find the axiom "knowledge is power" is only half true. It makes little difference how much "knowledge" a person accumulates if they do nothing with it. Knowledge, by definition, is limited because it only implies the *awareness* of facts, truths or principals. It does not involve the *application* of such things. It is decision—supported by action—which completes the equation. It is decision, backed by necessary action, which gives knowledge its significance. It is *decision*, backed by *sufficient action*, which defines our ultimate power.

The Action Formula

$$\text{Information} + \text{Action} = \text{Results}$$

The Value of This Book

The source of value you receive from the lessons contained in this book do not come from the information you read or the truths you learn. The value comes from the *application* of these things. In other words, there is nothing contained in these lessons which can help you—if you don't *choose* to help yourself. In order for the full benefit to be derived from these lessons, you must put them into practice. You must act on them—consistently—over time.

Decision Cannot Exist Without Action

A decision can be defined simply as "making a choice" or "the act of making up one's mind." Apart from action, however, decision has no meaning whatsoever. What is "deciding to go for a walk" if *you don't go for the walk?* People often make new years resolutions. Yet, most of these resolutions fail before the second month of the year. Why is this? One reason is because we often make decisions without supporting those decisions with sufficient action. Without the necessary action, decisions become void of all meaning.

Support Your Decisions With Sufficient Action

When you make a decision, any decision whatsoever, you must support that decision with sufficient action. Sufficient is to be understood as the amount of action necessary to accomplish the decision you make. If you have no intention of supporting your decisions with immediate and sufficient action, why make a decision in the first place? We often make decisions and postpone the action necessary to accomplish them because the conditions or circumstances are not "just right." But circumstances will never be "just right." If we wait for such conditions to present themselves the chances are very likely we will wait forever.

Mistakes Can Be Corrected

Another possible reason we delay action is because we fear the ramifications they may produce. We may make mistakes—we may fail. As a result, we often wait until we think we can perform our task flawlessly before we begin.

Again, if we believe such things, we are likely to wait forever. It is only through definite action that results may be created. But with all actions come possible failures and with all failures come learning experiences. Faulty or erroneous actions may be corrected in practice over time whereas *non-action* can only be remedied though *action*.

The Action Habit

The action habit may be defined as consistently supporting one's decisions with sufficient action, in order to, over time, develop a habit. Individuals who have developed the action habit arrive at decisions quickly and support those decisions with definite action. These individuals do not commit to making decisions unless they are absolutely sure they will support their decisions with action. As a result, they accomplish what they set out to accomplish. The action habit may be developed by consistently supporting one's decisions with action, over time, until a habit is developed. Action perpetuates itself.

The Non-Action Habit

The non-action habit may be defined as consistently supporting one's decisions with inaction or procrastination. Over time, just as consistent action produces a habit, so to does inaction and procrastination. Individuals who have developed the habit of non-action arrive at decisions without any thought of whether or not they will support them with action. As a result, they have many plans, but accomplish very little. The non-action habit is developed as a result of consistently failing to support one's decisions with sufficient action, until a habit of non-action or procrastination is developed. Non-action also perpetuates itself.

Someday Is Now

The only moment in time which really exists is *now*. Neither the past, nor the future really exist. The past is a memory of previous "now" moments. The future is a collection of potential "now" moments. But the only moment which truly exists is this one—*right now*. We often postpone our goals and dreams to the ambiguous "someday." The truth, however, is that *someday* is *now*. The only moment you will ever have is right *now*. Victory in *eternity* is victory in the *moment!* The question is *"to act or not to act?"*

The Ultimate Discipline

Before you make a decision, determine if you will support that decision with the action necessary to accomplish it. If not, decide *not* to do that which is before you. Discipline is nothing more than doing what you commit to do. It is nothing more than supporting your decisions with sufficient action. If you will not *actively* support the decisions you make, it is better to decide *not* to do something.

To Those Who Struggle With Decision Making

Many people struggle with making decisions. This often results from the fear of making "the wrong choice." Although no one wants to make "the wrong choice," it is better to make a decision than no decision at all. If it turns out our decision was wrong, we have the opportunity to learn something. We have the opportunity to gain new insight and understanding and learn from our "bad decision." On the other hand, if we avoid making decisions altogether, we will often paralyze ourselves with fear and become unable to decide on anything.

Selected Quotes

"Let him that would move the world first move himself."
-Socrates

"Immaturity is the incapacity to use one's intelligence without the guidance of another."
-Immanuel Kant

"Whatever you can do or dream you can, begin it. Boldness has genius, power, and magic in it."
-Goethe

"You can't build a reputation on what you're going to do"
-Henry Ford

"The road to failure and despair is littered with the dreams of those who failed to act."
-Napoleon Hill

"The great end of life is not knowledge but action."
-Thomas Henry Huxley

"Talent is cheaper than table salt. What separates the talented individual from the successful one is a lot of hard work and study."
-Stephen King

"To be is to do."
-Immanuel Kant

The Laws of Action and Results

1. Applied knowledge is power.
2. Decision cannot exist without action.
3. Non-action can only be corrected through action.
4. The only moment which truly exists is now.
5. Discipline is doing what you commit to do.
6. It is better to make a decision and learn from it than to make no decision at all.

Understanding Your Tendencies

1. How often do you procrastinate?
2. Do you do what you say?
3. Do you ever make plans for "someday"?
4. Do you need everything to be perfect before you begin something?
5. Do you ever avoid action for fear of failure?
6. How long does it normally take you to make a decision?
7. Do you talk a lot but accomplish very little?
8. Is the hardest part of a project "getting started"?

The Catalyst of Confidence

"Optimism is the faith that leads to achievement. Nothing can be done without hope and confidence."

-Helen Keller

Lesson XI: Confidence and Humility

The portrait of a person who understands and applies the ten previous lessons, consistently and over time, looks far different from that of a person who does not. Below you will find a portrait—in light of each lesson—of a person who has dedicated time and effort toward incorporating each lesson into their life on a consistent basis. This portrait—which is written in the form of a personal affirmation—may be used as a model to help you "see yourself as the person you would like to be."

I. Perception and Belief: I understand the affect my beliefs have on my perception of reality. I understand how my beliefs are created and strengthened. I perceive information in ways which benefit me. I have *consciously* rooted out my limiting beliefs. I have developed belief in my abilities. I understand *belief* gives me the power to *do*.

II. Choice and Initiative: My choices produce results and everything I do is a choice. I am the defining factor of my success or failure. I look to myself to solve problems. I respond to external circumstances in ways which benefit me. I see problems as opportunities to learn and grow.

III. Goals and Dreams: I know what I want. I have written goals. I have learned to *consistently* define, focus, believe, plan and act. I have seen my ideas become realities. I view the world in terms of my goals and dreams. I live my life with a vision.

IV. Thought and Concentration: I understand the affect my thoughts have on my actions and attitudes. I perceive information in ways which benefit me. I consciously seek to control the information I associate with. I strive to see myself as the person I would like to be.

V. Action and Habit: I understand habits and their elusive nature. I continuously work to identify and replace my bad habits. I consciously choose my actions, knowing over time that they will develop into habits. I understand I am a product of my habits.

VI. Fear and Action: I understand the process of conquering fear. When faced with fear: I focus on the action necessary to conquer my fear; I reinforce the belief that I-can-do-it; I visualize myself successfully completing the action necessary to overcome my fear; I act, in spite of my fear. I have developed the habit of responding to my fears with immediate action. I enjoy the fruits of an expanded comfort zone.

VII. Failure and Adversity: I understand the true nature of failure. I understand The Four Stages of Learning and view failure as an informative learning process. I have developed persistence which does not recognize failure. I have learned to disassociate myself from my failures. I visualize my success.

VIII. Self-Deception and Learning: I often deceive myself and constantly seek to identify my deceptions. I am honest with myself. I reflect on my actions and the consequences they produce. I seek to identify my beliefs which are based on assumptions. I consistently maintain the attitude of a student. I understand I don't know what I don't know.

IX. Emotion and Intelligence: I understand the great power my emotions have influencing my behavior and choices. I consistently seek an awareness of my emotional tendencies. I consciously respond to my emotions in ways which benefit me. I develop good habits.

X. Action and Results: I understand the importance of action. I reach decisions quickly and definitely. I consistently support my decisions with sufficient action and correct myself as I go. I have developed the action habit.

The Necessity of Hard Work and Progress

Confidence is a direct result of the consistent and proper *application* of the previous ten lessons. It is the *complete understanding** of these lessons which reveal to us the reality of human potential. It is these lessons, when *applied* in collaboration, *consistently* over time, which form *The Catalyst of Confidence*. Incorporating the previous lessons into our lives requires work—hard work. The lessons are simple, but are not always easy to apply. As a result of our work and persistence, we will begin to see progress, both in ourselves and in reaching our goals. Seeing progress in our lives, both internally and externally, confirms our faith in our abilities and ultimately culminates in a genuine state of confidence. Without *hard work* and *visible progress*, our confidence can only remain an intellectual endeavor and can neither be fully realized or understood.

The Confidence Formula

Hard Work → Progress → Confidence

---

* As explained in the *Introduction*, to fully understand any given subject, it must be understood on both an intellectual and functional basis. Thus, each lesson must be understood in this way to properly result in genuine confidence.

A Proper Understanding of Confidence

The consistent application of the previous ten lessons, collaboratively over time, will result in a remarkably powerful state of confidence. Confidence, as properly defined, accents faith in oneself and one's abilities without any suggestion of *conceit* or *arrogance*. It is important to understand the complete polarity between confidence and the negative attributes of pride (such as *conceit* or *arrogance*) which are commonly associated with it. Pride reveals itself through a variety of forms, such as showing off; seeking credit; constant correcting; the inability to admit wrongs—none of which should be associated with confidence. The difference between *acting confident* and *being confident* is self-evident. True confidence stresses faith in oneself and one's abilities *without* the need to assert it.

The Keystone of Confidence

Confidence recognizes possibility, it reveals our capacity to comprehend reality and see the potential and possibility for good, i.e., to solve everyday challenges or problems and pursue goals and dreams. Yet it is only through the acknowledgment and awareness of our limits (our deceptions) that we may truly come to understand what we are capable of. Despite the necessity of the previous lessons, it is *humility* which defines the most vital component of confidence. Humility, as properly defined, is the acknowledgment of truth. It is knowing you don't know everything. It is knowing you have limits. It is knowing you have faults. Humility is maintaining a perpetual attitude of a student, exactly as discussed in *Lesson VIII: Self-Deception and Learning*. It is only through developing a strong sense of *humility*, that we may truly come to recognize our potential.

The Qualified Yes

Confidence is *not* blind optimism. As previously stated, confidence accents faith in oneself and one's abilities—it is a *qualified* faith in one's decisions. It is the ability to say *yes*; *no*; *I don't know*; *I can*; *I can't*—with competence and understanding. Confidence, like humility, is the realization of truth. It is the realization of both our limits *and* potential, of our strengths *and* weaknesses. When we understand our failures, we are better able to understand our success. When we understand *"no—I can't"* we understand *"yes—I can!"*

The Crown of Confidence

The attainment of genuine confidence creates an attitude of *magnanimity*, which can be defined as generosity in forgiveness, freedom from resentfulness, high mindedness, or nobility of disposition. Stated another way, the magnanimous person is not bound to the trivialities of everyday life which haunt the masses of mankind. Narrow irritations, annoyances, gossips, slander, or petty arguments are of no interest to them. They literally do not notice the narrow-minded problems of the majority. They are consumed by the process of pursuing their objectives. They are not indifferent, but *choose* not to be burdened by the mediocrity of life.

The Laws of Confidence and Humility

1. Confidence is the result of the consistent

application of the first ten lessons.
2. Hard work and visible progress are necessary to develop confidence.
3. Confidence emphasizes faith in oneself without any suggestion of conceit or arrogance.
4. The most vital element of confidence is humility.
5. When individuals understand their limits they are better able to understand their potential.
6. Magnanimity is the direct result of true confidence.

Understanding Your Tendencies

1. Have you taken the time and effort to incorporate the previous lessons into your life?
2. Do you work hard or do enough just to get by?
3. Have you taken time to measure the internal and external progress in your life?
4. Do you actively *apply* the previous lessons on a *consistent* basis?
5. What lessons do you struggle with?
    - What can you do to better incorporate these lessons into your life?

The World's Your Oyster

"The analytical power should not be confounded with simple ingenuity; for while the analyst is necessarily ingenious, the ingenious man is often remarkably incapable of analysis."

-Edgar Allen Poe

Lesson XII: Possibility and Impossibility

The World's Your Oyster

The most precious gift you will ever receive is your life—it is an immeasurable opportunity. The very fabric of life itself is permeated with possibility and potential. It is a blank canvas which *must* be painted upon. It is a block of marble which *will* be chiseled and defined by the great sculptor. Life is opportunity, possibility, potential. And sooner or later you must realize that life—your life—is what you make it: the world is your oyster.

The Ultimate Paradox

Described below are three historical events. They each share a common trait: they describe a human achievement which was at one time believed to be impossible.

> On December 17th 1903, brothers Orville and Wilbur Wright successfully tested a heavier-than-air machine that could fly. For thousands of years man had been haunted by the possibility of flying. Many people held the belief that "if we were meant to fly, God would have given us wings." Newspapers dismissed the event as fabrication. Years passed before the general population came to believe the historic flight actually took place.
>
> On May 29th 1953, friends Edmund Hilary and Tenzing Norgay, stood on the summit of Mt. Everest—the highest point on the face of the earth. The summit, standing at 29,029 feet, had eluded the grasp of mankind for centuries. All previous attempts had ended in failure. Numerous climbers had disappeared—only to be found frozen solid by other adventurers. Many questioned mankind's ability to reach the summit, let alone survive the

climb down.

On May 6th 1954, Roger Bannister, a 25 year old medical student from Oxford, ran a mile in 3 minutes and 59.4 seconds. At the time, a four minute mile was commonly seen as a physical impossibility. Scientists believed the capacities of the human bone structure, lungs and heart were insufficient to sustain the endurance that would be required. Journalists attended the May 6th run expecting new material to chronicle yet another Bannister failure.

What we find (after *analyzing* events such as these within their historical context) is that nearly every major achievement mankind has been involved in was commonly *believed* to be completely impossible until *after it was accomplished.* We find that the individuals who accomplish the impossible, believe that the *"impossible" is possible*.

The General Idea of Impossible

Impossible refers to something which is *not able to be done*. A proper understanding, however, takes into account the reality that most "impossibilities" are relative to their time and place *and* are often wholly dependent upon the *beliefs* of the people within that specific time and place.

Logical Impossibilities

With respect to the previous paragraph, it must be mentioned that things do exist which are impossible. The fact that you may believe that 1 + 1 = 3 cannot change the fact that 1 + 1 = 2. Similarly, no one could draw a circle which is a square, just as nothing can exist and not exist simultaneously. These are examples of logical impossibilities.

Analyzing What You Believe

When we *analyze* our beliefs and develop a mature understanding of them, we realize that both impossible and possible are creations of our minds. They are often only true because we *believe* they are true. Yes, things exist which are impossible, wholly independent of what we believe. But the limits we often place on ourselves are not logical impossibilities. We may be confronted with problems and situations which we believe are hopeless—things which we believe we can do nothing to correct. Yet it is the *belief* that a situation is hopeless which enables the situation to *actually be hopeless*. As described in *Lesson I: Perception and Belief:* your beliefs determine your reality *and* your potential.

Beyond Impossible

Perhaps most things we take for granted today were once believed to be impossible. As we have seen, it was at one time commonly believed that no one could build a machine that could fly, climb Mount Everest, or run a mile in less than four minutes. But we have found that the individuals who accomplish the impossible *believe* that the *impossible is possible*. It appears that the only way to determine that which is truly possible, is to enter the realm of the impossible.

The World's Your Oyster

When it comes to your ability to live the life you want, very few things exist which can stop you. The next time you communicate to yourself "I can't do—," "—is impossible," or "—is hopeless," realize these are not statements which correspond to objective reality. You must recognize the truth. Your potential to accomplish the things you desire, to solve problems, build relationships or communicate effectively, *is determined by what you believe*. The possibility or impossibility of a given object is contingent upon your own beliefs. Without belief, almost nothing is possible. With belief, almost anything is possible. Your life is what you make it. Why not make the life you want?

Selected Quotes

"Who said it could not be done? And what great victories has he to his credit which qualify him to judge others accurately?"
-Napoleon Hill

"Impossible is a word only to be found in the dictionary of fools."
-Napoleon Bonaparte

"Whether you believe you can or you can't, you're right."
-Henry Ford

"Throughout the centuries there were men who took first steps down new roads armed with nothing but their own vision."
-Ayn Rand

The World's Your Oyster

*"If we all did the things we are capable of,
we would astound ourselves."*
-Thomas Edison

*"Heroism is never rational and every heroic life and
death is a challenge to cool reason's pronouncing
that it is folly to attempt the impossible."*
-Edith Hamilton

*"Whatever the mind of man can conceive and
believe the mind of man can achieve."*
-Napoleon Hill

"No! No different! Only different in your mind!"
-Yoda

The Laws of Possibility and Impossibility

1. Your life is an immeasurable opportunity.
2. Those who accomplish the impossible believe it is possible.
3. Limiting beliefs only exist in one's mind.
4. Individuals are capable of creating the life they desire.

Understanding Your Tendencies

1. Are you aware of your beliefs?
2. How often do you use the world "impossible"?
3. Do you ever tell yourself you can't do something?
4. Have you allowed the opinions of others to determine what you can or cannot do?
5. Are you *currently* working to create the life you want?

Formulas

"Every formula which expresses a law of nature is a hymn of praise to God."

-Maria Mitchell

Appendix: A

Formulas

The "Understanding" Formula (p. *xvii*)

Intellectual + Functional = Understanding (Complete)

The Belief Formula (p. 24)

Information → Perception → Repetition → Belief

The Self-Image Formula (p. 25)

Beliefs → Self-Image → Reality/Potential

The Volition Formula (p. 31)

Stimulus → (Choice) → Response

The Response Formula (p. 34)

External Circumstances → Reactive or Active

The Dream Formula (p. 41)

Define → Focus → Believe → Plan → Act
(Mental Creation → Material Creation)

The Information Formula (p. 49)

Information → Thinking

The Thought/Action Formula (p. 50)

Information → Thinking → Action

The Habit Formula (p. 59)

Action (Mental/Physical) → Habit → Result (You/Life)

The Complete Formula (p. 59)

Information → Thinking → Actions → Habits → Results

The Fear Formula (p. 66)

Action > Fear

The Emotion Formula (p. 94)

Emotion → Response

The Emotional Intelligence Formula (p. 95)

Emotion → (Choice) → Response
(Stimulus → Choice → Response)

The Action Formula (p. 101)

Information + Action = Results

The Confidence Formula (p. 111)

Hard Work → Progress → Confidence

Laws

"The future begins today, not tomorrow."

-Pope John Paul II

Appendix: B

The Laws of Intellectual and Functional Understanding (p. *xviii*)

1. Genuine understanding is comprised of both intellectual and functional components.

The Laws of Perception and Belief (p. 26)

1. Actions presuppose belief.
2. Beliefs are created, strengthened and nurtured by oneself.
3. Beliefs govern action.
4. Beliefs determine one's perception of reality.
5. Beliefs determine one's potential.
6. Beliefs may be changed.
7. Beliefs are developed and changed through the perception and repetition of information.

The Laws of Choice and Initiative (p. 36)

1. Individuals possess the ability to take action: to solve problems and direct their life.
2. Everything one does is a choice.
3. Through choice and action individuals determine their success and failure.
4. Between stimulus and response is choice.
5. Choice determines one's response to external circumstances.

The Laws of Goals and Dreams (p. 44)

1. All things begin as thoughts.
2. All accomplishment presupposes desire.
3. The starting point of all achievement is defining

what one wants.
4. All objectives are realized through the conscious or unconscious application of a five-step process.

The Laws of Thought and Concentration (p. 52)

1. The mind is one's greatest asset.
2. The mind operates according to the information it concentrates upon.
3. Individuals are continuously influenced by their environment.
4. The substance of information is positive or negative.
5. Information is subordinate to perception.
6. Dominating thoughts result from the information an individual concentrates upon.
7. Action and behavior is the result of one's dominating thoughts.
8. Individuals emulate the qualities they admire and concentrate upon.
9. Individuals possess the ability to control the information they associate with.

The Laws of Action and Habit (p. 61)

1. A habit is an action performed subconsciously.
2. Nearly all actions stem from habit.
3. One's habits result from the repetition of actions.
4. Habits are created and controlled by the subconscious section of the mind.
5. The subconscious mind is not guided by morality.
6. Individuals are the product of their habits.
7. Individuals have the power to change their habits.

The Laws of Fear and Action (p. 70)

1. Fear is an emotional state-of-mind which inhibits one's ability to take action.
2. An individual experiences fear when they move beyond their comfort zone.
3. The more a fear is avoided the more power it has over an individual.
4. Action conquers fear.
5. Overcoming fears expands one's comfort zone.

The Laws of Failure and Adversity (p. 79)

1. Failure is the worlds greatest educational process.
2. Persistence despite failure results in success.
3. Visualizing one's success helps one succeed.
4. Problems are opportunities.
5. An individual is not their failures.
6. There is no failure, there are only results.

The Laws of Self-Deception and Learning (p. 89)

1. Self-deception is the act of misleading oneself.
2. All individuals deceive themselves.
3. Self-deception reveals itself through one's choices and beliefs.
4. Being honest with oneself is critical to identify one's deceptions.
5. Deceptions are identified through reflecting on one's experiences and questioning one's beliefs.
6. There is always more to learn.

The Laws of Emotion and Intelligence (p. 97)

1. Emotions are thoughts linked to feelings.
2. Emotions are powerful forces in influencing one's behavior.
3. Individuals have developed habits in how they respond to their emotions, many of which developed during childhood.
4. Emotional intelligence is the ability to respond to emotions in ways which benefit oneself.
5. Emotional intelligence can be developed.
6. The goal of developing emotional intelligence is to develop new habits.

The Laws of Action and Results (p. 106)

1. Applied knowledge is power.
2. Decision cannot exist without action.
3. Non-action can only be corrected through action.
4. The only moment which truly exists is now.
5. Discipline is doing what you commit to do.
6. It is better to make a decision and learn from it than to make no decision at all.

The Laws of Confidence and Humility (p. 113)

1. Confidence is the result of the consistent application of the first ten lessons.
2. Hard work and visible progress are necessary to develop confidence.
3. Confidence emphasizes faith in oneself without any suggestion of conceit or arrogance.
4. The most vital element of confidence is humility.
5. When individuals understand their limits they are

better able to understand their potential.
6. Magnanimity is the direct result of true confidence.

The Laws of Possibility and Impossibility (p. 121)

1. Your life is an immeasurable opportunity.
2. Those who accomplish the impossible believe it is possible.
3. Limiting beliefs only exist in one's mind.
4. Individuals are capable of creating the life they desire.

Lexicon

"You will know the truth and the truth will set you free."

-John 8:32

Appendix: C

Lexicon

Action: The process of acting or doing. Action is the most vital component of success and the only remedy for non-action. Action trumps inaction because fallacious actions may be remedied while inaction may only be corrected through action. Without action nothing can be accomplished.

Action, Mental: All conscious thoughts, including analytical and critical thinking, perceptions, visualizations, emotions and emotional responses to stimuli.

Action, Physical: All physical actions performed by a person.

Active: Concerning external circumstances, individuals respond in one of two ways: by being Active or Reactive. Active responses are characterized by a strong sense of personal accountability while examining what can be done to improve the situation and/or oneself. This approach often results in a greater level of self-awareness and control.

Activity, Blind: The process of working or "staying busy" while simultaneously ignoring the results or lack of results being produced.

Application: The process of assimilating information and using or applying it in a practical or beneficial way.

Attitude: The state of mind of an individual. Attitudes have a powerful affect upon actions as they are closely linked with emotions.

Belief: A thought habit which governs action. A personal representation of reality which governs one's behavior. Beliefs determine how a person perceives reality as well as what they are capable of accomplishing.

Beliefs, Arrogant: A deceptive belief characterized by overrating one's own opinions or abilities. Often characterized by an inability to admit faults. Arrogant beliefs are *believed* to be true despite being false.

Beliefs, Limiting: A deceptive belief characterized by undervaluing one's own opinions, abilities or potential. Generally a limiting belief is only true because it is *believed* to be true.

Catalyst: Something which causes or accelerates an activity or state of being.

Change: The ability to alter reality, i.e., to progress and improve or solve problems.

Choice: The ability to act deliberately; to master impulses and desires; to subdue instincts and emotions.

Comfort Zone: An area of personality characterized by a lack of anxiety, tension or fear which as been created by one's habits. By definition, fears and anxieties lie beyond one's comfort zone.

Confidence: A state of mind characterized by a strong faith in oneself and one's abilities without any suggestion of conceit or arrogance. Confidence reveals one's capacity to comprehend reality and see the potential and possibility for good. It is closely linked with Humility because it is only through knowing one's limits that an individual may truly come to know their potential.

Concentration: The ability to focus one's mind on specific objects or information—consistently—over a period of time. Concentration is responsible for the creation of an individuals dominating thoughts and is required to solve problems and help bring goals and dreams into reality. When associated with a defined objective (a goal or dream), concentration enables new ideas to develop which enable plans to be created.

Decision: The ability to act deliberately; to master impulses and desires; to subdue instincts and emotions.

Discipline: The ability to do what one commits to do.

Doubt: A perception of the mind characterized by a lack of faith in oneself. Doubt most often results from inaction and indecision.

Dream: A defined object of desire and the starting point of any achievement. The ability to conceive beyond one's immediate reality and work to bring such conceptions into being. Dreams provide purpose and direction to one's life.

Emotion: A thought predominantly linked to a feeling, i.e., love, joy, anger, etc. Perhaps the most powerful force in influencing behavior. Emotions are habitual responses to specific information or stimuli, much of which have been carried over from one's childhood.

Emotional Intelligence: Responding to one's emotions—especially negative emotions—in ways which benefit rather than inhibit, i.e., using one's emotions intelligently.

Lexicon 137

Emotional intelligence is a skill which can be developed and is based on the law of habit.

Environment: The information perceived by an individual from external circumstances, conditions and influences. Most notably one's family, close friends and interests. Environment has an enormous influence on an individual because it provides the majority of the information perceived. However, it should be said that the defining factor of a persons behavior is not the environment itself, but rather, how a person responds to their environment.

Experience: A knowledge or understanding developed from one's perceptions of information or stimuli encountered in life.

External Circumstances: Everything which exists beyond one's self. External circumstances describe the world around us which we have no direct control over. We can, however, control how we respond.

Failure: A perception of the mind. Objectively there is no such thing as failure, there are only results. Failure only exists if it is perceived and accepted as failure.

Fear: A negative emotion which breeds indecision, procrastination and inaction. Fears may be overcome through action.

Focus: The ability to concentrate one's mind on a specific object—consistently—over a period of time. Focus is required to solve problems and help bring goals and dreams into reality.

Lexicon

Goal: A defined objective attached to a specific date or time-frame for its attainment. See also: *Dream*.

Habit: A subconscious action, i.e., an action (mental or physical) performed without conscious realization. Habits are created by the subconscious section of the mind.

Habit, Action: The habit of supporting one's decisions with sufficient action. Individuals who have developed this habit reach decisions quickly and support them with immediate and sufficient action. As a consequence, they tend to accomplish what they have set out to accomplish.

Habit, Non-Action: The habit of not supporting decisions with action. Individuals who have developed this habit reach decisions thoughtlessly and rarely act on them. They may naturally have many plans but accomplish very little.

Humility: The acknowledgment of truth. Humility is based on the knowledge and awareness of one's limits. It is an acceptance that one is not perfect and has access to limited information at any given time. Humility is maintained through a continuous attitude of a student.

Idea: Information which reaches the conscious mind, generally from the subconscious, which is directed toward the attainment of some end. Ideas provide us with the raw material needed for planning.

Impossibility: Something which is not able to be done. Things termed "impossibilities" are generally relative to a time and place and are often wholly dependent on the *beliefs* of the individuals within that time and place.

Lexicon 139

Impossibility, Logical: Something which cannot happen by virtue of its very nature. For example, a circle cannot be a square.

Indecision: The habit of being unable to decide. Indecision often results from a fear and/or the inertia from a developed habit of indecision.

Information: The building block of creation and the fuel of the mind. It is the defining factor of thought, action and habit. The essence of changing one's life is changing the information one associates with.

Information, Negative: Information which does not improve one's life, causes or prolongs problems, or hinders one's ability to accomplish goals and dreams.

Information, Positive: Information which improves one's life, helps solve problems, or increases one's ability to accomplish goals and dreams.

Initiative: The ability to consciously *choose* to take action, in order to solve problems, change and improve one's life or progress toward goals and dreams.

Intelligence: The ability to apply information in a practical or beneficial way.

Limits: Things which are beyond one's capacity to do. For example, no person may know all there is to know about a given subject.

Magnanimity: A character of personality or state of mind which ultimately results from genuine confidence in oneself. A magnanimous attitude can be seen in the ability to forgive generously; freedom from negative emotions such as pettiness, anger, hatred, jealousy, or resentfulness and an overall nobility of disposition.

Mind, Conscious: The conscious mind describes the awareness of one's thoughts, emotions and attitudes and is the only section of the mind which is under an individuals direct control. Information enters the conscious mind through the senses.

Mind, Subconscious: The section of mind which classifies, stores, and implements all information held by the conscious mind. The subconscious is "programmed" with the information it receives from the conscious. It observes an individuals every action (such as perceptions, thoughts, and responses) in order to produce habits. The speed at which the subconscious operates is greatly influenced by *emotion*. The stronger an emotion, the faster it responds.

Opportunity: A perception of the mind which enables individuals to solve problems, change, improve or reach goals and dreams.

Perception: An individual's attempt to discern reality or apprehend information (stimuli) which provides the blueprint for one's beliefs. Perception often wields the most power in influencing one's life because it allows the transformation of information. In other words, a person has the power to change positives into negatives and negatives into positives.

Plans: The perceived necessary steps to accomplish something. Often resulting from ideas which flash into the conscious mind due to proper concentration or focus. Plans which prove faulty may always be corrected as new ideas always present themselves insofar as individuals continues their efforts in focusing on their objectives.

Possibility/Potential: That which could exist but does not yet. An individuals potential is often solely determined by their perceptions and beliefs.

Power: Applied information. Information cannot be useful without application, just as decisions cannot exist without action.

Premise: The underlying foundations, presumptions or basis for anything. Belief is said to be the ultimate premise because all action stems from belief.

Problems: Conditions, circumstances or situations in life which provide individuals with opportunities to learn and grow.

Procrastination: The delaying or avoidance of action. Procrastination often develops into a strong non-action habit which may only be remedied through action.

Ramifications: The consequences of a given action or non-action.

Reactive: Concerning external circumstances, individuals respond in one of two ways: by being Active or Reactive. Individuals who are Reactive allow circumstances to control their actions and feelings. Reactive responses are characterized by a general lack of personal accountability (blaming and excuses) and are often accompanied by a

142 Lexicon

victim mentality. This approach is highly dangerous. If developed into a strong habit it may result in an individuals complete loss of free will.

Reality, Objective: The way things actually are. Facts.

Reality, Subjective: The way individuals perceive things to be. Opinions.

Repetition: The performing of an action (or non-action) over and over again. Repetition is necessary in developing skills and habits.

Response: An individual's ability to deliberately respond to what happens to them. Responses are a function of personal initiative, choice and decision.

Results: Feedback, which reveals the virtue of one's actions, i.e., perceptions, thoughts, habits, plans, etc.

Self-Awareness: The awareness of one's own thoughts, emotions, actions, habits or tendencies in the moment they occur.

Self-Control/Management: The ability to act deliberately as opposed to reacting spontaneously.

Self-Deception: Betraying one's ultimate self-interest through the act of misleading oneself in one's choices or beliefs.

Self-Discipline: An individuals habit of doing what they commit to do.

Lexicon 143

Self-Image: A psychological blueprint or image of oneself which is created by one's beliefs, i.e., an individuals opinion of their own value.

Self-Interest: One's ultimate good.

Self-Reliance: The ability to rely on oneself in one's actions and decisions.

Skill: An ability which may be acquired through persistent concentration, effort and determination.

Someday Syndrome: The habit of expecting things to happen "someday" rather than working toward them today.

Stimuli: Information which enters the conscious mind prior to being interpreted by one's perceptions, i.e., raw information, facts.

Success: The progressive realization of a goal or dream.

Thoughts, Conscious: Thoughts of which an individual is aware.

Thoughts, Dominating: The information an individual thinks in terms of and/or makes decisions based on. Dominating thoughts result from the information an individual concentrates upon. The substance of one's dominating thoughts may be positive or negative, helpful or harmful, etc.

Thoughts, Emotionalized: Thoughts which are linked to strong feelings. Emotionalized thoughts (whether positive or negative) are more easily recognized by the subconscious mind.

Thoughts, Magnetic: A characteristic of all thoughts. Each thought "held" in one's mind (whether positive or negative) will attract to it additional thoughts of a similar or related nature. Emotionalized thoughts are the most "magnetic."

Transformation: An individuals ability to change what information (circumstances, situations, results, etc.) means to oneself through perception. For example, changing a negative result into a positive learning experience.

Understanding (Complete): To know or understand something on an intellectual and functional basis.

Understanding, Functional: Knowledge or understanding attained from action and experience. Such as learning by doing.

Understanding, Intellectual: Knowledge or understanding attained from academic or theoretical pursuits.

Visualization: To mentally see something. Visualizations can be used to aid oneself in nearly all situations. As a basic rule of thumb, individuals tend to become what they see themselves becoming and do what they see themselves doing. Visualizations also help an individual focus on a defined goal or dream.

Sources

"You will be the same in five years as you are today except for the people you meet and the books you read."

-Charlie "T" Jones

Appendix: D

Sources

Allen, James. *As A Man Thinketh*. New York: Grosset & Dunlap, n.d.

Arbinger Institute. *Leadership and Self-Deception*. San Francisco: Berrett-Koehler, 2000.

Aquinas, Thomas. *Selected Writings*. London: Penguin Books, 1998.

Bradberry, Travis and Greaves, Jean. *The Emotional Intelligence Quick Book*. New York: Simon & Schuster, 2005.

Covey, Stephen R. *The 7 Habits of Highly Effective People: Powerful Lessons in Personal Change*. New York: Simon & Schuster, 1989.

Dyer, Wayne W. *Your Erroneous Zones*. New York: HarperCollins, 1993.

Emerson, Ralph Waldo. *The Essential Writings of Ralph Waldo Emerson*. New York: Random House, 2000.

Frankl, Viktor E. *Man's Search For Meaning*. Boston: Beacon Press, 1959.

Helmstetter, Shad. *What To Say When You Talk To Yourself*. New York: Simon & Schuster, 1982.

Hill, Napoleon. *Think and Grow Rich*. New York: Random House, 1937.

Kiyosaki, Robert T. *If You Want To Be Rich and Happy Don't Go To School?* Fairfield: Aslan Publishing, 1992.

Maltz, Maxwell. *Psycho-Cybernetics*. New York: Simon & Schuster, 1960.

Maxwell, John C. *Failing Forward: Turning Mistakes Into Stepping Stones For Success.* Nashville: Thomas Nelson, 2000.

NLP Comprehensive. *NLP: The New Technology of Achievement*. New York: HarperCollins, 1994.

Pilzer, Paul Zane. *Unlimited Wealth: The Theory and Practice of Economic Alchemy.* New York: Crown Publishing Group, 1990.

Robbins, Anthony. *Unlimited Power: The New Science of Personal Achievement*. New York: Simon & Schuster, 1986.

Schwartz, David J. *The Magic of Thinking Big*. New York: Prentice-Hall, 1959.

Stone, W. Clement. *The Success System That Never Fails.* Wise: The Napoleon Hill Foundation, 2004.

von Hildebrand, Dietrich. *Transformation In Christ*. San Francisco: Ignatius Press, 2001.

von Mises, Ludwig. *Human Action: A Treatise on Economics.* New Haven: Yale University, 1949.

Waitley, Denis. *The Psychology of Winning*. New York: Berkley Publishing Group, 1979.

Get articles, case studies and ask questions at
www.catalystofconfidence.com

About The Author

Ken Parsell is an independent educator, writer and philomath, best known for his highly interactive and discussion oriented teaching style. He is a strong proponent of accelerated teaching techniques, which encompass Auditory, Visual, and Kinesthetic learning. Ken is founder and president of Noble One, an institute for privately funded research and development which focuses on the functional application of ideas, including many found in Philosophy, Psychology, Economics, Education, and Leadership. He lives in Michigan with his family.

Notes:

Notes:

Notes:

Notes: